Marketing Your Business
with CoPilot

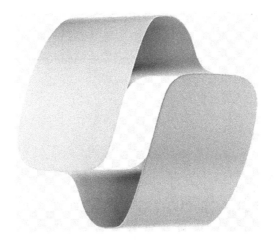

by Terry C Power

Table of Contents

Introduction to CoPilot and Modern Marketing

In the digital age, marketing has evolved beyond traditional methods, demanding more sophisticated tools and techniques to reach and engage customers. Among these modern tools, CoPilot stands out as a revolutionary AI-driven marketing assistant, designed to streamline and enhance various aspects of marketing efforts. This book is your comprehensive guide to understanding and utilizing CoPilot to its full potential, transforming your marketing strategies and ultimately driving your business growth.

The Evolution of Marketing

Marketing has come a long way from its roots in simple print advertisements and word-of-mouth recommendations. The advent of the internet and social media has transformed how businesses interact with their customers. Today, marketing is about building relationships, engaging with audiences in real-time, and delivering personalized experiences. This shift has brought about the need for tools that can handle complex data, provide actionable insights, and automate repetitive tasks—enter CoPilot.

What is CoPilot?

CoPilot is an advanced AI-powered marketing tool designed to assist businesses in automating and optimizing their marketing efforts. By leveraging artificial intelligence, CoPilot can analyze large volumes of data, identify trends, and provide recommendations that help businesses make informed decisions. From content creation and social media management to email marketing and analytics, CoPilot covers a wide range of functions that are essential for modern marketing.

Why CoPilot?

The primary advantage of using CoPilot lies in its ability to save time and resources while increasing the effectiveness of marketing campaigns. Traditional marketing strategies often involve a significant amount of manual work, from researching and creating content to scheduling posts and analyzing performance metrics. CoPilot automates these processes, allowing marketers to focus on more strategic tasks such as planning and creative development.

Key Features of CoPilot

1. **Content Generation**: CoPilot can create high-quality content tailored to your brand's voice and audience preferences. Whether you need

blog posts, social media updates, or email newsletters, CoPilot generates engaging content quickly and efficiently.

2. **Social Media Management**: Schedule and manage your social media posts across multiple platforms from a single dashboard. CoPilot helps you maintain a consistent online presence without the hassle of manual scheduling.

3. **Email Marketing**: Design and automate personalized email campaigns that resonate with your subscribers. CoPilot's AI analyzes your audience's behavior and preferences to optimize email delivery times and content.

4. **Analytics and Reporting**: Gain insights into your marketing performance with detailed analytics and reports. CoPilot tracks key metrics, such as engagement rates, conversion rates, and ROI, providing you with the information needed to refine your strategies.

5. **Customer Segmentation**: Understand your audience better by segmenting them based on demographics, behavior, and preferences. This allows for more targeted and effective marketing campaigns.

The Importance of AI in Marketing

Artificial intelligence is not just a buzzword; it's a powerful tool that is transforming industries across the globe. In marketing, AI helps businesses make sense of vast amounts of data, predict customer behavior, and deliver personalized experiences at scale. By automating routine tasks, AI frees up valuable time for marketers to focus on strategy and creativity, leading to more innovative and effective campaigns.

How This Book Will Help You

This book is structured to take you through the journey of integrating CoPilot into your marketing efforts. Each chapter delves into a specific aspect of using CoPilot, providing practical tips, detailed instructions, and real-world examples to illustrate its effectiveness. By the end of this book, you will have a solid understanding of how to leverage CoPilot to enhance your marketing strategies and drive business growth.

Whether you are a small business owner looking to streamline your marketing processes or a seasoned marketer seeking to stay ahead of the curve, this book is your ultimate guide to mastering marketing with CoPilot. So, let's embark on this journey together and unlock the full potential of AI-powered marketing.

Chapter 1:

Introduction to CoPilot and Modern Marketing

Introducing CoPilot

CoPilot is an advanced AI-powered marketing assistant designed to help businesses streamline their marketing efforts. By automating routine tasks and providing actionable insights, CoPilot allows marketers to focus on more strategic and creative aspects of their work. Whether you are a small business owner or a marketing professional, CoPilot can help you enhance your marketing strategies and achieve better results.

Key Features of CoPilot

1. **Content Generation**: CoPilot can create high-quality content tailored to your brand's voice and audience preferences. Whether you need blog posts, social media updates, or email newsletters, CoPilot generates engaging content quickly and efficiently.

2. **Social Media Management**: Schedule and manage your social media posts across multiple platforms from a single dashboard. CoPilot helps you maintain a consistent online presence without the hassle of manual scheduling.

3. **Email Marketing**: Design and automate personalized email campaigns that resonate with your subscribers. CoPilot's AI analyzes your audience's behavior and preferences to optimize email delivery times and content.

4. **Analytics and Reporting**: Gain insights into your marketing performance with detailed

analytics and reports. CoPilot tracks key metrics, such as engagement rates, conversion rates, and ROI, providing you with the information needed to refine your strategies.

5. **Customer Segmentation**: Understand your audience better by segmenting them based on demographics, behavior, and preferences. This allows for more targeted and effective marketing campaigns.

Benefits of Using CoPilot

The primary advantage of using CoPilot lies in its ability to save time and resources while increasing the effectiveness of marketing campaigns. Traditional marketing strategies often involve a significant amount of manual work, from researching and creating content to scheduling posts and analyzing performance metrics. CoPilot automates these processes, allowing marketers to focus on more strategic tasks such as planning and creative development.

Another key benefit of CoPilot is its ability to deliver personalized experiences at scale. Personalization is crucial in modern marketing, as consumers expect brands to understand their preferences and deliver relevant content. CoPilot's AI-driven insights enable businesses to create personalized messages that resonate with their audience, leading to higher engagement and conversion rates.

The Future of Marketing with CoPilot

As technology continues to advance, the role of AI in marketing will only become more significant. CoPilot represents the future of marketing, where AI-driven tools will play a central role in helping businesses connect with their customers. By automating routine tasks, providing actionable insights, and enabling personalized interactions, CoPilot empowers marketers to create more effective and engaging campaigns.

Conclusion

In this book, we will explore the various features and capabilities of CoPilot, providing you with practical tips and strategies to enhance your marketing efforts. From setting up CoPilot for your business to leveraging advanced techniques and analyzing performance metrics, this comprehensive guide will help you unlock the full potential of AI-powered marketing. Whether you are new to CoPilot or looking to deepen your understanding, this book will equip you with the knowledge and skills needed to succeed in the ever-evolving world of digital marketing.

So, let's embark on this journey together and discover how CoPilot can revolutionize your marketing strategies and drive your business growth.

The Challenges of Modern Marketing

While the opportunities presented by digital marketing are vast, they come with their own set of challenges. The sheer volume of data generated by online interactions can be overwhelming, making it difficult for marketers to sift through and find actionable insights. Additionally, the rapid pace of technological change means that marketers must continuously learn and adapt to new tools and platforms.

Another significant challenge is maintaining consistency across multiple marketing channels. With audiences spread across social media, email, websites, and other platforms, ensuring a cohesive message and brand experience can be daunting. CoPilot addresses these challenges by providing a centralized platform that integrates various marketing activities, making it easier to maintain consistency and streamline operations.

How CoPilot Works

CoPilot leverages artificial intelligence and machine learning to automate and optimize marketing tasks. Here's a closer look at how CoPilot works:

1. **Data Collection and Analysis**: CoPilot collects data from various sources, including your website, social media accounts, and email campaigns. It then analyzes this data to identify trends, patterns, and opportunities.

2. **Content Creation**: Using natural language processing (NLP) and other AI techniques, CoPilot generates high-quality content that aligns with your brand's voice and messaging. This content can be customized to suit different platforms and audience segments.

3. **Automation**: CoPilot automates routine tasks such as scheduling social media posts, sending email campaigns, and generating reports. This frees up time for marketers to focus on strategy and creativity.

4. **Optimization**: CoPilot continuously monitors the performance of your marketing activities and provides recommendations for optimization. This includes suggestions for improving engagement rates, targeting specific

audience segments, and adjusting content based on performance metrics.

5. **Personalization**: By analyzing customer behavior and preferences, CoPilot helps you deliver personalized experiences that resonate with your audience. This includes personalized email content, targeted social media ads, and customized website experiences.

Getting Started with CoPilot

To get started with CoPilot, you'll need to set up an account and connect your marketing channels. Here's a step-by-step guide to help you get up and running:

1. **Sign Up**: Visit the CoPilot website and sign up for an account. You'll need to provide some basic information about your business and marketing goals.

2. **Connect Your Channels**: Once your account is set up, you'll need to connect your marketing channels. This includes your social media accounts, email marketing platform, and website analytics. CoPilot provides easy-to-follow instructions for connecting each channel.

3. **Define Your Goals**: Before you start using CoPilot, it's important to define your marketing

goals. Are you looking to increase brand awareness, generate leads, or drive sales? Clear goals will help CoPilot tailor its recommendations to your specific needs.

4. **Explore the Dashboard**: Familiarize yourself with the CoPilot dashboard, where you can access all of your marketing data, content, and automation tools. The dashboard provides a centralized view of your marketing activities, making it easy to manage and optimize your campaigns.

5. **Create Your First Campaign**: Start by creating a simple marketing campaign. CoPilot's intuitive interface guides you through the process, from selecting your target audience to designing your content and scheduling your posts. As you become more comfortable with the platform, you can explore more advanced features and techniques.

Real-World Applications of CoPilot

To illustrate the power of CoPilot, let's look at a few real-world applications:

1. **E-commerce**: An online retailer uses CoPilot to automate their email marketing campaigns. By

analyzing customer purchase history and behavior, CoPilot generates personalized product recommendations and sends targeted emails to drive repeat purchases. The retailer sees a significant increase in open rates and conversion rates, leading to higher revenue.

2. **Content Marketing**: A blog uses CoPilot to generate content ideas and optimize their publishing schedule. CoPilot analyzes trending topics and audience engagement metrics to suggest blog post topics that are likely to resonate with readers. The blog's traffic and engagement metrics improve as a result of more relevant and timely content.

3. **Social Media**: A small business uses CoPilot to manage their social media presence. CoPilot schedules and posts content across multiple platforms, monitors engagement, and provides insights into the best times to post and the types of content that perform best. The business sees an increase in followers and engagement, helping them build a stronger online community.

Conclusion

The landscape of marketing is continually evolving, and businesses must adapt to stay competitive. CoPilot offers a powerful solution to the challenges of modern marketing, providing AI-driven tools that automate tasks, optimize strategies, and deliver personalized experiences. By integrating CoPilot into your marketing efforts, you can save time, increase efficiency, and achieve better results.

This book will guide you through the process of setting up and using CoPilot, offering practical tips, detailed instructions, and real-world examples. Whether you are new to CoPilot or looking to deepen your understanding, this comprehensive guide will equip you with the knowledge and skills needed to succeed in the ever-evolving world of digital marketing.

Next Steps

In the following chapters, we will delve deeper into the specific features and capabilities of CoPilot. From setting up your account and connecting your marketing channels to leveraging advanced techniques and analyzing performance metrics, you'll learn everything you need to know to master marketing with CoPilot. So, let's continue this journey and unlock the full potential of AI-powered marketing.

Chapter 2:

Setting Up CoPilot for Your Business

In this chapter, we will walk you through the process of setting up CoPilot for your business. From creating your account to configuring your settings and connecting your marketing channels, you'll learn how to get started with CoPilot and tailor it to your specific needs.

Creating Your CoPilot Account

The first step in setting up CoPilot is to create an account. Here's how to do it:

1. **Visit the CoPilot Website**: Go to the CoPilot website and click on the "Sign Up" button. You'll be prompted to enter your email address and create a password.

2. **Provide Business Information**: Next, you'll need to provide some basic information about your business. This includes your business

name, industry, and size. This information helps CoPilot tailor its recommendations to your specific needs.

3. **Confirm Your Email**: After entering your information, you'll receive a confirmation email. Click on the link in the email to verify your account and complete the sign-up process.

Configuring Your Settings

Once your account is set up, you'll need to configure your settings. Here are the key settings to consider:

1. **Business Profile**: Fill out your business profile with detailed information about your brand, including your logo, tagline, and mission statement. This helps CoPilot understand your brand's identity and tailor its content recommendations accordingly.

2. **Marketing Goals**: Define your marketing goals within CoPilot. Are you looking to increase brand awareness, generate leads, or drive sales? Setting clear goals will help CoPilot provide more relevant recommendations and track your progress over time.

3. **Content Preferences**: Customize your content preferences by specifying the types of content

you want to generate (e.g., blog posts, social media updates, email newsletters) and the tone and style that best represent your brand.

4. **Notification Settings**: Configure your notification settings to receive alerts and updates from CoPilot. You can choose to receive notifications via email or within the CoPilot dashboard.

Connecting Your Marketing Channels

To fully leverage CoPilot's capabilities, you'll need to connect your marketing channels. Here's how to do it:

1. **Social Media Accounts**: Connect your social media accounts (e.g., Facebook, Twitter, Instagram, LinkedIn) to CoPilot. This allows CoPilot to schedule and manage your posts, as well as analyze engagement metrics. Follow the prompts to authorize CoPilot to access your accounts.

2. **Email Marketing Platform**: If you use an email marketing platform (e.g., Mailchimp, Constant Contact), connect it to CoPilot. This enables CoPilot to design and automate your email campaigns. You'll need to provide your API key or login credentials to establish the connection.

3. **Website Analytics**: Connect your website analytics platform (e.g., Google Analytics) to CoPilot. This allows CoPilot to track your website traffic, user behavior, and conversion rates. Follow the instructions to integrate your analytics account with CoPilot.

Exploring the CoPilot Dashboard

Once your settings are configured and your marketing channels are connected, you can start exploring the CoPilot dashboard. Here are some key features to familiarize yourself with:

1. **Overview**: The overview section provides a snapshot of your marketing performance, including key metrics such as engagement rates, conversion rates, and ROI. This helps you quickly assess the effectiveness of your campaigns.

2. **Content Library**: The content library stores all the content generated by CoPilot, including blog posts, social media updates, and email newsletters. You can browse, edit, and organize your content from this section.

3. **Campaigns**: The campaigns section allows you to create, manage, and track your marketing

campaigns. You can set up new campaigns, monitor their progress, and analyze their performance using detailed reports.

4. **Automation**: The automation section enables you to set up automated workflows for tasks such as scheduling social media posts, sending email campaigns, and generating reports. This helps you streamline your marketing processes and save time.

5. **Analytics**: The analytics section provides in-depth insights into your marketing performance. You can track key metrics, such as engagement rates, conversion rates, and ROI, and use this information to optimize your strategies.

Creating Your First Campaign

Now that you're familiar with the CoPilot dashboard, it's time to create your first campaign. Here's a step-by-step guide to help you get started:

1. **Define Your Objectives**: Start by defining the objectives of your campaign. Are you looking to increase brand awareness, generate leads, or drive sales? Clear objectives will help you measure the success of your campaign.

2. **Select Your Target Audience**: Identify the target audience for your campaign. Who are you trying to reach? Consider factors such as demographics, interests, and behavior. CoPilot can help you segment your audience based on this information.

3. **Create Your Content**: Use CoPilot's content generation tools to create high-quality content for your campaign. Whether you need blog posts, social media updates, or email newsletters, CoPilot can generate engaging content tailored to your brand's voice and audience preferences.

4. **Schedule Your Posts**: Schedule your social media posts and email campaigns using CoPilot's automation tools. This ensures that your content is delivered at the optimal times for maximum engagement.

5. **Monitor and Optimize**: Track the performance of your campaign using CoPilot's analytics and reporting tools. Monitor key metrics such as engagement rates, conversion rates, and ROI, and use this information to optimize your strategy.

Conclusion

Setting up CoPilot for your business is the first step towards transforming your marketing efforts. By creating an account, configuring your settings, and connecting your marketing channels, you'll be ready to leverage CoPilot's powerful AI-driven tools to automate tasks, optimize strategies, and deliver personalized experiences. In the next chapter, we'll delve into understanding your audience and how CoPilot can help you segment and target your audience for more effective marketing campaigns.

Chapter 3:

Understanding Your Audience

In marketing, understanding your audience is crucial to creating effective campaigns. Knowing who your customers are, what they want, and how they behave allows you to tailor your messages and strategies to resonate with them. In this chapter, we will explore how CoPilot helps you understand your audience and use this knowledge to create more targeted and successful marketing campaigns.

The Importance of Audience Understanding

Understanding your audience goes beyond basic demographics. It involves gaining insights into their preferences, behaviors, and motivations. This deeper understanding allows you to:

1. **Personalize Your Marketing**: Deliver messages that speak directly to your audience's needs and interests, increasing engagement and conversion rates.

2. **Improve Targeting**: Identify and target the right audience segments, ensuring that your marketing efforts reach the most relevant and receptive individuals.

3. **Enhance Customer Experience**: Create a more enjoyable and seamless experience for your customers by anticipating their needs and preferences.

4. **Increase ROI**: By targeting the right audience with the right messages, you can achieve better results with fewer resources, improving your return on investment (ROI).

Audience Segmentation

One of the key features of CoPilot is its ability to segment your audience based on various criteria. Audience segmentation involves dividing your customer base into distinct groups based on characteristics such as demographics, behavior, and preferences. This allows you to create more targeted and relevant marketing campaigns. Here's how CoPilot helps with audience segmentation:

1. **Demographic Segmentation**: Segment your audience based on demographic factors such as age, gender, income, education, and location. This helps you tailor your messages to the specific needs and preferences of different demographic groups.

2. **Behavioral Segmentation**: Segment your audience based on their behavior, such as purchase history, website interactions, and engagement with your marketing content. This allows you to target customers who are more likely to respond to your campaigns.

3. **Psychographic Segmentation**: Segment your audience based on their attitudes, values, interests, and lifestyles. This helps you create messages that resonate with the underlying motivations and preferences of your audience.

4. **Geographic Segmentation**: Segment your audience based on their geographic location. This allows you to tailor your marketing efforts to specific regions, considering local preferences and trends.

Using CoPilot to Understand Your Audience

CoPilot provides several tools and features to help you understand your audience and create targeted marketing campaigns. Here's how to leverage these tools:

1. **Customer Profiles**: CoPilot creates detailed customer profiles by collecting and analyzing data from various sources. These profiles include demographic information, purchase history, behavior patterns, and preferences, giving you a comprehensive view of your customers.

2. **Audience Insights**: CoPilot analyzes your audience data to provide insights into their behavior and preferences. This includes identifying trends, such as popular products, peak engagement times, and common customer journeys.

3. **Segmentation Tools**: CoPilot's segmentation tools allow you to divide your audience into distinct groups based on various criteria. You can create custom segments and save them for use in your marketing campaigns.

4. **Personalization**: CoPilot uses AI to deliver personalized content and recommendations to different audience segments. This includes personalized email content, targeted social media ads, and customized website experiences.

Practical Tips for Audience Understanding

To get the most out of CoPilot's audience understanding tools, consider the following practical tips:

1. **Collect Comprehensive Data**: Ensure that you are collecting data from all relevant sources, including your website, social media accounts, email campaigns, and customer interactions. The more data you have, the better CoPilot can understand your audience.

2. **Regularly Update Your Segments**: Audience preferences and behaviors can change over time. Regularly review and update your

audience segments to ensure that your marketing efforts remain relevant and effective.

3. **Test and Iterate**: Use A/B testing to experiment with different messages and strategies for your audience segments. Analyze the results and iterate based on what works best.

4. **Leverage Customer Feedback**: Incorporate customer feedback into your audience understanding efforts. This includes reviews, surveys, and direct interactions with your customers.

Conclusion

Understanding your audience is a critical component of effective marketing. By leveraging CoPilot's powerful tools and features, you can gain deeper insights into your customers' preferences, behaviors, and motivations. This knowledge allows you to create more targeted and personalized marketing campaigns, improving engagement, conversion rates, and ROI. In the next chapter, we will explore how to create a content strategy that aligns with your audience's needs and preferences.

Chapter 4: Creating a Content Strategy

Content is at the heart of modern marketing. It's how you communicate with your audience, convey your brand's message, and drive engagement. In this chapter, we will explore how to create a content strategy that aligns with your audience's needs and preferences, leveraging CoPilot's tools to generate high-quality, targeted content.

The Importance of a Content Strategy

A well-defined content strategy is essential for several reasons:

1. **Consistency**: A content strategy ensures that your messaging is consistent across all channels, which is crucial for building a strong brand identity.

2. **Relevance**: By understanding your audience and planning your content accordingly, you can create content that is relevant and valuable to your audience.

3. **Efficiency**: A content strategy helps you plan and schedule your content in advance, saving time and resources.

4. **Measurement**: A content strategy allows you to set clear goals and metrics for your content,

making it easier to measure its effectiveness and optimize your efforts.

Developing Your Content Strategy

Here are the key steps to developing a content strategy:

1. **Define Your Goals**: Start by defining the goals of your content strategy. Are you looking to increase brand awareness, generate leads, drive sales, or engage your audience? Clear goals will guide your content creation and help you measure success.

2. **Understand Your Audience**: Use the insights gained from CoPilot to understand your audience's needs, preferences, and behaviors. This will help you create content that resonates with them.

3. **Identify Key Topics and Themes**: Based on your audience insights, identify the key topics and themes that are most relevant to your audience. Consider their pain points, interests, and questions.

4. **Create a Content Calendar**: Plan your content in advance by creating a content calendar. This includes scheduling blog posts, social media

updates, email newsletters, and other content types. A content calendar ensures consistency and helps you stay organized.

5. **Determine Content Types**: Decide on the types of content you will create, such as blog posts, videos, infographics, podcasts, and social media updates. Consider what formats work best for your audience and goals.

6. **Allocate Resources**: Determine the resources needed to execute your content strategy, including budget, tools, and personnel. Ensure that you have the necessary resources to create and distribute high-quality content.

7. **Measure and Optimize**: Set clear metrics to measure the effectiveness of your content, such as engagement rates, traffic, conversions, and ROI. Regularly analyze your performance and optimize your strategy based on the insights gained.

Using CoPilot to Create Content

CoPilot provides several tools to help you create high-quality, targeted content:

1. **Content Generation**: CoPilot uses AI to generate content based on your brand's voice

and audience preferences. This includes blog posts, social media updates, email newsletters, and more.

2. **Content Suggestions**: CoPilot analyzes trending topics and audience engagement metrics to suggest content ideas that are likely to resonate with your audience.

3. **Content Scheduling**: Use CoPilot's automation tools to schedule your content in advance. This ensures that your content is delivered at the optimal times for maximum engagement.

4. **Content Optimization**: CoPilot provides recommendations for optimizing your content, including suggestions for improving headlines, adding keywords, and enhancing readability.

Practical Tips for Content Creation

To create effective content with CoPilot, consider the following practical tips:

1. **Align Content with Goals**: Ensure that each piece of content aligns with your overall marketing goals. For example, if your goal is to generate leads, include clear calls to action and lead capture forms.

2. **Focus on Quality**: Quality is more important than quantity. Focus on creating high-quality content that provides value to your audience. This includes well-researched, informative, and engaging content.

3. **Be Consistent**: Consistency is key to building a strong brand presence. Stick to your content calendar and maintain a consistent posting schedule.

4. **Use Visuals**: Incorporate visuals such as images, videos, and infographics into your content. Visuals help to capture attention and convey information more effectively.

5. **Engage with Your Audience**: Encourage your audience to engage with your content by asking questions, inviting comments, and responding to feedback. This helps to build a community around your brand.

Conclusion

Creating a content strategy is essential for delivering consistent, relevant, and high-quality content that resonates with your audience. By leveraging CoPilot's powerful tools, you can streamline your content creation process, optimize your efforts, and achieve better results. In the next chapter, we will explore how to leverage social media for marketing success, using CoPilot to manage and optimize your social media presence.

Leveraging Social Media for Marketing Success

Social media is a powerful tool for connecting with your audience, building brand awareness, and driving engagement. In this chapter, we will explore how to leverage social media for marketing success, using CoPilot to manage and optimize your social media presence.

Chapter 5: Leveraging Social Media for Marketing Success

Social media platforms offer unparalleled opportunities for businesses to engage with their audience, build brand loyalty, and drive sales. However, managing a successful social media strategy requires more than just posting regularly. It involves understanding your audience, creating engaging content, and leveraging analytics to refine your approach. CoPilot can assist in every step of this process, making it easier to achieve your social media marketing goals.

The Importance of Social Media Marketing

Social media marketing is essential for several reasons:

1. **Increased Brand Awareness**: Social media platforms have billions of active users, providing a vast audience for your brand.

2. **Customer Engagement**: Social media allows for direct interaction with customers, fostering a sense of community and loyalty.

3. **Cost-Effective Marketing**: Compared to traditional advertising, social media marketing can be more cost-effective, offering higher returns on investment.

4. **Real-Time Feedback**: Social media provides immediate feedback from customers, allowing for quick adjustments to your marketing strategy.

5. **Traffic and Conversions**: Effective social media strategies can drive significant traffic to your website and increase conversion rates.

Setting Up Your Social Media Profiles

Before diving into content creation and engagement, it's crucial to set up your social media profiles correctly. Here's how to do it:

1. **Consistent Branding**: Ensure that your branding is consistent across all social media platforms. This includes using the same logo, color scheme, and tone of voice.

2. **Complete Profiles**: Fill out all profile information thoroughly, including your bio, website link, and contact details. A complete profile looks professional and helps build trust with your audience.

3. **High-Quality Visuals**: Use high-quality images for your profile picture and cover photo. Visuals are often the first impression visitors have of your brand on social media.

4. **Optimized Descriptions**: Write clear and engaging descriptions that reflect your brand's personality and highlight what makes your business unique. Use relevant keywords to improve discoverability.

Creating Engaging Social Media Content

Creating engaging content is key to building a strong social media presence. Here are some tips for creating content that resonates with your audience:

1. **Know Your Audience**: Use the audience insights provided by CoPilot to understand

what types of content your audience prefers. Tailor your content to meet their interests and needs.

2. **Mix Content Types**: Diversify your content by mixing different types such as images, videos, infographics, and articles. This keeps your feed interesting and engaging.

3. **Tell Stories**: Use storytelling to connect with your audience on an emotional level. Share behind-the-scenes content, customer stories, and brand milestones.

4. **Use Visuals**: High-quality visuals are more likely to capture attention. Use striking images, engaging videos, and well-designed graphics.

5. **Interactive Content**: Encourage interaction by creating polls, quizzes, and contests. Interactive content can boost engagement and make your audience feel more involved with your brand.

6. **User-Generated Content**: Share content created by your customers, such as reviews, photos, and testimonials. This not only provides social proof but also encourages other customers to engage with your brand.

Scheduling and Automating Posts with CoPilot

Consistency is key in social media marketing. CoPilot's scheduling and automation features can help ensure that your posts go out regularly and at optimal times. Here's how to make the most of these features:

1. **Content Calendar**: Use CoPilot to create a content calendar. Plan your posts in advance, ensuring a consistent posting schedule that aligns with your marketing goals.

2. **Optimal Posting Times**: CoPilot analyzes your audience's engagement patterns to recommend the best times to post. Schedule your content to be published at these optimal times to maximize reach and engagement.

3. **Automated Posting**: Set up automated posting for your social media content. This saves time and ensures that your posts go out even when you're not online.

4. **Content Variations**: Create different variations of your posts for different platforms. CoPilot can help tailor your content to suit the specific requirements and audiences of each social media platform.

Engaging with Your Audience

Engagement is a crucial aspect of social media marketing. Here's how to effectively engage with your audience:

1. **Respond to Comments**: Take the time to respond to comments on your posts. This shows that you value your audience's input and helps build a sense of community.

2. **Monitor Mentions**: Use CoPilot to monitor mentions of your brand across social media. Respond to positive mentions to show appreciation and address any negative feedback promptly.

3. **Join Conversations**: Participate in relevant conversations and trending topics. This increases your visibility and positions your brand as an active participant in your industry.

4. **Encourage User Interaction**: Ask questions, invite opinions, and encourage your audience to share their thoughts. This increases engagement and helps you gather valuable insights about your customers.

5. **Use Hashtags**: Incorporate relevant hashtags into your posts to increase discoverability.

Research trending and industry-specific hashtags that your audience is likely to follow.

Analyzing and Optimizing Your Social Media Strategy

Analyzing the performance of your social media efforts is essential for continuous improvement. CoPilot provides robust analytics tools to help you track and optimize your strategy. Here's how to use these tools:

1. **Track Key Metrics**: Monitor key metrics such as engagement rates, follower growth, click-through rates, and conversions. These metrics provide insights into what's working and what needs improvement.

2. **Analyze Content Performance**: Use CoPilot to analyze the performance of your individual posts. Identify which types of content perform best and adjust your strategy accordingly.

3. **A/B Testing**: Conduct A/B tests to compare different versions of your posts. Experiment with different headlines, images, and calls to action to see what resonates most with your audience.

4. **Optimize Posting Schedule**: Review the performance of your posts at different times and days. Adjust your posting schedule based on when your audience is most active.

5. **Benchmark Against Competitors**: Use CoPilot to benchmark your social media performance against your competitors. This helps you identify areas where you can improve and stay ahead of industry trends.

Conclusion

Leveraging social media for marketing success requires a strategic approach that includes understanding your audience, creating engaging content, maintaining consistency, and continuously analyzing performance. CoPilot offers powerful tools to streamline these processes, making it easier to manage and optimize your social media presence. In the next chapter, we will explore how to create and manage effective email marketing campaigns using CoPilot.

Chapter 6: Creating Effective Email Marketing Campaigns

Email marketing remains one of the most effective ways to reach your audience, nurture leads, and drive conversions. In this chapter, we will explore how to create and manage effective email marketing campaigns, leveraging CoPilot's tools to optimize your efforts and achieve better results.

The Benefits of Email Marketing

Email marketing offers several advantages:

1. **Direct Communication**: Email allows you to communicate directly with your audience, delivering personalized messages to their inbox.

2. **High ROI**: Email marketing has one of the highest returns on investment (ROI) of any marketing channel, making it a cost-effective strategy.

3. **Nurturing Leads**: Email is an excellent tool for nurturing leads through the sales funnel, providing valuable content and building relationships over time.

4. **Measurable Results**: Email marketing platforms provide detailed analytics, allowing you to track the performance of your campaigns and make data-driven decisions.

5. **Automation**: Email marketing can be automated, saving time and ensuring timely delivery of your messages.

Building Your Email List

A successful email marketing campaign starts with a high-quality email list. Here's how to build and grow your email list:

1. **Sign-Up Forms**: Use sign-up forms on your website, blog, and social media profiles to collect email addresses. Ensure that your forms are easy to find and fill out.

2. **Lead Magnets**: Offer lead magnets such as eBooks, whitepapers, checklists, and webinars in exchange for email addresses. Ensure that your lead magnets provide value to your audience.

3. **Landing Pages**: Create dedicated landing pages with compelling offers to capture email addresses. Use clear calls to action and optimize your pages for conversions.

4. **Social Media**: Promote your email list on social media by sharing sign-up forms and lead magnets. Encourage your followers to join your list for exclusive content and updates.

5. **Events**: Collect email addresses at events such as webinars, trade shows, and conferences. Use sign-up sheets or digital forms to capture contact information.

Crafting Compelling Email Content

Creating compelling email content is key to engaging your audience and achieving your marketing goals. Here are some tips for crafting effective email content:

1. **Personalization**: Use personalization to address recipients by name and tailor your content to their interests and preferences. CoPilot can help you segment your audience and personalize your emails.

2. **Compelling Subject Lines**: Write attention-grabbing subject lines that entice recipients to open your emails. Keep them concise, clear, and relevant to the content.

3. **Clear and Concise Content**: Keep your email content clear and concise. Use short paragraphs, bullet points, and subheadings to make your emails easy to read.

4. **Engaging Visuals**: Incorporate visuals such as images, videos, and graphics to enhance your

email content. Visuals can make your emails more engaging and memorable.

5. **Strong Calls to Action**: Include clear and compelling calls to action (CTAs) that guide recipients to take the desired action, such as clicking a link, downloading a resource, or making a purchase.

6. **Mobile Optimization**: Ensure that your emails are optimized for mobile devices. A significant portion of email opens occurs on mobile, so your emails should be easy to read and navigate on smaller screens.

Automating Your Email Campaigns

Automation is a powerful feature of email marketing that can save time and improve efficiency. Here's how to leverage automation with CoPilot:

1. **Welcome Series**: Set up an automated welcome series to greet new subscribers and introduce them to your brand. Provide valuable content and set expectations for future emails.

2. **Drip Campaigns**: Create drip campaigns to nurture leads over time. Drip campaigns deliver a series of emails at predetermined intervals, guiding recipients through the sales funnel.

3. **Behavioral Triggers**: Use behavioral triggers to send automated emails based on specific actions taken by recipients, such as website visits, link clicks, or abandoned carts.

4. **Re-engagement Campaigns**: Set up re-engagement campaigns to win back inactive subscribers. Send automated emails with special offers or incentives to encourage re-engagement.

5. **Birthday and Anniversary Emails**: Use automation to send personalized birthday and anniversary emails to your subscribers. These emails can include special offers and personalized messages.

Measuring and Optimizing Your Email Campaigns

Analyzing the performance of your email campaigns is crucial for continuous improvement. CoPilot provides robust analytics tools to help you track and optimize your email marketing efforts. Here's how to use these tools:

1. **Track Key Metrics**: Monitor key metrics such as open rates, click-through rates, conversion rates, and unsubscribe rates. These metrics

provide insights into the effectiveness of your campaigns.

2. **A/B Testing**: Conduct A/B tests to compare different versions of your emails. Test elements such as subject lines, content, visuals, and CTAs to see what resonates most with your audience.

3. **Analyze Engagement**: Use CoPilot to analyze how recipients engage with your emails. Identify which links are clicked most often, which content is most popular, and where recipients drop off.

4. **Optimize Send Times**: Review the performance of your emails at different times and days. Adjust your send times based on when your audience is most likely to engage.

5. **Segment and Personalize**: Use CoPilot's segmentation tools to create more targeted and personalized email campaigns. Tailor your content to the specific needs and preferences of different audience segments.

Conclusion

Creating effective email marketing campaigns involves building a high-quality email list, crafting compelling content, leveraging automation, and continuously analyzing and optimizing your efforts. CoPilot offers powerful tools to streamline these processes, making it easier to achieve your email marketing goals. In the next chapter, we will explore how to optimize your website for better performance and higher conversions, using CoPilot to identify opportunities and implement improvements.

Chapter 7: Optimizing Your Website for Better Performance and Higher Conversions

Your website is the central hub of your online presence. It's where visitors learn about your brand, explore your products or services, and take action, whether that's making a purchase, signing up for your newsletter, or contacting you for more information. Optimizing your website for performance and conversions is crucial for turning visitors into customers. In this chapter, we will explore how to use CoPilot to identify opportunities for improvement and implement strategies to enhance your website's performance and conversion rates.

The Importance of Website Optimization

Website optimization is essential for several reasons:

1. **User Experience**: A well-optimized website provides a better user experience, which can lead to higher engagement and satisfaction.

2. **SEO Performance**: Search engines favor optimized websites, which can improve your search rankings and drive more organic traffic to your site.

3. **Conversion Rates**: Optimizing your website for conversions helps turn visitors into leads or customers, increasing your overall ROI.

4. **Loading Speed**: Faster websites provide a better user experience and can significantly reduce bounce rates.

Key Elements of Website Optimization

To optimize your website effectively, focus on the following key elements:

1. **Performance Optimization**: Improve your website's loading speed and overall performance.
2. **SEO Optimization**: Ensure your website is search engine-friendly to improve your rankings and visibility.
3. **Conversion Rate Optimization (CRO)**: Enhance your website's ability to convert visitors into customers.

Performance Optimization

Website performance plays a crucial role in user experience and SEO. Here's how to optimize your website's performance:

1. **Improve Loading Speed**: Use tools like Google PageSpeed Insights or GTmetrix to analyze your website's loading speed and identify areas for improvement. Common recommendations include optimizing images, leveraging browser caching, and minimizing JavaScript and CSS.

2. **Mobile Optimization**: Ensure your website is fully optimized for mobile devices. Use responsive design to provide a seamless experience across different screen sizes.

3. **Optimize Images**: Compress and resize images to reduce loading times without sacrificing quality. Use image formats like WebP for better compression.

4. **Minimize HTTP Requests**: Reduce the number of HTTP requests by combining files, using CSS sprites, and minimizing the use of plugins and third-party scripts.

5. **Enable Compression**: Use Gzip or Brotli compression to reduce the size of your website's files, improving loading speed.

SEO Optimization

Search engine optimization is essential for driving organic traffic to your website. Here's how to optimize your website for SEO:

1. **Keyword Research**: Use CoPilot's keyword research tools to identify relevant keywords for your industry. Optimize your website's content, meta tags, and URLs with these keywords.

2. **Quality Content**: Create high-quality, valuable content that addresses your audience's needs and interests. Use CoPilot's content generation tools to produce SEO-friendly blog posts, articles, and landing pages.

3. **On-Page SEO**: Optimize your website's on-page elements, including title tags, meta descriptions, header tags, and image alt text. Ensure that each page is optimized for a specific keyword.

4. **Internal Linking**: Use internal links to guide visitors through your website and improve the distribution of link equity. This helps search engines understand the structure of your site.

5. **Backlinks**: Build high-quality backlinks from reputable websites to improve your domain

authority and search rankings. CoPilot can help you identify potential backlink opportunities.

Conversion Rate Optimization (CRO)

Conversion rate optimization focuses on enhancing your website's ability to convert visitors into customers. Here's how to optimize your website for conversions:

1. **Clear CTAs**: Ensure that your calls to action (CTAs) are clear, compelling, and prominently displayed. Use action-oriented language that encourages visitors to take the desired action.

2. **Landing Pages**: Create dedicated landing pages for specific campaigns or offers. Use CoPilot to design and test different variations of your landing pages to determine which performs best.

3. **A/B Testing**: Conduct A/B tests to compare different versions of your website's pages, headlines, images, and CTAs. Use CoPilot's A/B testing tools to identify the most effective elements.

4. **Social Proof**: Incorporate social proof elements such as customer testimonials, reviews, case

studies, and trust badges. These elements can build trust and encourage visitors to convert.

5. **User-Friendly Design**: Ensure that your website's design is intuitive and easy to navigate. Use clear menus, logical page structures, and a consistent design throughout your site.

6. **Forms and Checkout Process**: Simplify your forms and checkout process to reduce friction and increase conversions. Only ask for essential information and use progress indicators to guide users through the process.

Using CoPilot for Website Optimization

CoPilot offers several tools and features to help you optimize your website:

1. **Analytics and Reporting**: Use CoPilot's analytics tools to track key performance metrics such as page load times, bounce rates, and conversion rates. Analyze this data to identify areas for improvement.

2. **SEO Tools**: CoPilot provides SEO tools to help you conduct keyword research, analyze your website's SEO performance, and identify optimization opportunities.

3. **A/B Testing**: Use CoPilot's A/B testing tools to experiment with different website elements and determine which variations yield the best results.

4. **Content Generation**: Leverage CoPilot's content generation tools to create high-quality, SEO-friendly content that resonates with your audience.

5. **Performance Monitoring**: CoPilot monitors your website's performance and provides alerts for any issues that may impact user experience or SEO.

Practical Tips for Website Optimization

To get the most out of CoPilot's website optimization tools, consider the following practical tips:

1. **Regular Audits**: Conduct regular audits of your website to identify and fix performance issues, SEO gaps, and conversion barriers.

2. **Stay Updated**: Keep up with the latest trends and best practices in website optimization. CoPilot's tools and resources can help you stay informed and implement the latest strategies.

3. **User Feedback**: Collect and analyze user feedback to identify pain points and areas for improvement. Use surveys, feedback forms, and user testing to gather insights.

4. **Continuous Improvement**: Optimization is an ongoing process. Continuously monitor your website's performance and make data-driven improvements to enhance user experience and conversions.

Conclusion

Optimizing your website for better performance and higher conversions is crucial for achieving your marketing goals. By leveraging CoPilot's powerful tools and features, you can identify opportunities for improvement, implement effective strategies, and continuously refine your approach. In the next chapter, we will explore how to use CoPilot to manage and optimize your online advertising campaigns for maximum impact.

Chapter 8: Managing and Optimizing Online Advertising Campaigns

Online advertising is a powerful way to reach a broader audience, drive traffic to your website, and generate leads and sales. However, managing and optimizing online advertising campaigns can be complex and time-consuming. In this chapter, we will explore how to use CoPilot to streamline your online advertising efforts, maximize your return on investment (ROI), and achieve better results.

The Importance of Online Advertising

Online advertising offers several benefits:

1. **Reach**: Online ads allow you to reach a large and diverse audience across various platforms and devices.

2. **Targeting**: Advanced targeting options enable you to reach specific demographics, interests, and behaviors, increasing the relevance and effectiveness of your ads.

3. **Measurable Results**: Online advertising platforms provide detailed analytics, allowing you to track the performance of your campaigns and make data-driven decisions.

4. **Flexibility**: Online ads can be easily adjusted and optimized in real-time, allowing you to respond quickly to changing market conditions and audience preferences.

5. **Cost-Effective**: With proper management and optimization, online advertising can be a cost-effective way to generate leads and sales, providing a high ROI.

Setting Up Your Online Advertising Campaigns

To set up successful online advertising campaigns, follow these steps:

1. **Define Your Goals**: Start by defining the objectives of your campaigns. Are you looking to increase brand awareness, drive traffic, generate leads, or boost sales? Clear goals will guide your strategy and help you measure success.

2. **Identify Your Target Audience**: Use CoPilot's audience insights to identify the demographics, interests, and behaviors of your target audience. This information will help you create highly targeted and relevant ads.

3. **Choose Your Platforms**: Decide which platforms to advertise on, such as Google Ads, Facebook Ads, Instagram Ads, LinkedIn Ads, or other relevant networks. Consider where your audience spends their time and which platforms align with your goals.

4. **Create Compelling Ad Creative**: Develop high-quality ad creative that captures attention and communicates your message effectively. Use CoPilot's content generation tools to create engaging headlines, ad copy, and visuals.

5. **Set Your Budget**: Determine your advertising budget and allocate it across your chosen platforms and campaigns. Use CoPilot's budget management tools to monitor and optimize your spending.

Optimizing Your Online Advertising Campaigns

Optimization is key to maximizing the effectiveness of your online advertising campaigns. Here's how to optimize your campaigns using CoPilot:

1. **Keyword Optimization**: For search ads, conduct thorough keyword research to identify relevant and high-performing keywords. Use CoPilot's keyword tools to optimize your keyword list and improve your ad targeting.

2. **Audience Targeting**: Refine your audience targeting based on performance data. Use CoPilot to analyze audience insights and adjust your targeting criteria to reach the most relevant and responsive segments.

3. **Ad Copy and Creative**: Continuously test and optimize your ad copy and creative. Use A/B testing to compare different versions of your ads and identify the most effective elements.

4. **Bid Management**: Monitor and adjust your bids to ensure you are getting the best value for your budget. Use CoPilot's bid management tools to automate bid adjustments based on performance data.

5. **Landing Page Optimization**: Ensure that your landing pages are optimized for conversions. Use CoPilot's tools to analyze landing page performance and implement improvements to increase conversion rates.

6. **Monitor and Analyze Performance**: Regularly review your campaign performance using CoPilot's analytics tools. Track key metrics such as click-through rates (CTR), conversion rates, cost per click (CPC), and return on ad spend (ROAS).

7. **Retargeting**: Implement retargeting campaigns to reach visitors who have interacted with your website but have not yet converted. Use CoPilot to set up and optimize retargeting ads to re-engage these potential customers.

Practical Tips for Online Advertising Success

To get the most out of your online advertising campaigns, consider the following practical tips:

1. **Stay Updated on Trends**: Keep up with the latest trends and best practices in online advertising. CoPilot provides resources and insights to help you stay informed and ahead of the competition.

2. **Leverage Automation**: Use CoPilot's automation features to streamline your campaign management. Automation can save time and improve efficiency, allowing you to focus on strategy and optimization.

3. **Budget Flexibility**: Be flexible with your budget and adjust it based on performance. Allocate more budget to high-performing campaigns and pause or reduce spending on underperforming ones.

4. **Test Continuously**: Always be testing different elements of your campaigns, from ad copy and creative to targeting and bidding strategies. Continuous testing and optimization are key to long-term success.

5. **Analyze Competitor Strategies**: Use CoPilot to analyze your competitors' advertising strategies. Identify what's working for them and consider how you can apply similar tactics to your own campaigns.

Conclusion

Managing and optimizing online advertising campaigns requires a strategic approach, continuous testing, and data-driven decision-making. By leveraging CoPilot's powerful tools and features, you can streamline your efforts, maximize your ROI, and achieve better results. In the next chapter, we will explore how to use CoPilot to enhance your customer relationship management (CRM) efforts, building stronger relationships and driving customer loyalty.

Chapter 9: Enhancing Customer Relationship Management (CRM) with CoPilot

Customer relationship management (CRM) is at the heart of every successful business. It involves managing interactions with existing and potential customers to build strong relationships, increase customer loyalty, and drive business growth. In this chapter, we will explore how to use CoPilot to enhance your CRM efforts, streamline customer interactions, and provide exceptional customer service.

The Importance of CRM

Effective CRM is essential for several reasons:

1. **Customer Retention**: Building strong relationships with customers increases loyalty and reduces churn rates.

2. **Customer Satisfaction**: Providing excellent customer service enhances satisfaction and encourages positive word-of-mouth referrals.

3. **Sales Growth**: Understanding customer needs and preferences helps you tailor your sales strategies and increase conversions.

4. **Data-Driven Decisions**: CRM systems provide valuable data that can inform business decisions and improve overall efficiency.

Key Elements of CRM

To enhance your CRM efforts, focus on the following key elements:

1. **Customer Data Management**: Collecting, storing, and analyzing customer data to gain insights and inform strategies.

2. **Customer Segmentation**: Dividing your customer base into segments based on specific criteria to deliver more personalized experiences.

3. **Communication and Engagement**: Maintaining regular, meaningful communication with customers through various channels.

4. **Customer Support**: Providing timely and effective support to address customer issues and concerns.

5. **Feedback and Improvement**: Gathering and analyzing customer feedback to continuously improve products and services.

Using CoPilot for CRM

CoPilot offers several tools and features to enhance your CRM efforts:

1. **Centralized Customer Data**: CoPilot's CRM system allows you to centralize all customer data, including contact information, interaction

history, and purchase behavior. This comprehensive view helps you understand your customers better and tailor your interactions accordingly.

2. **Customer Segmentation**: Use CoPilot to segment your customer base into different groups based on demographics, behavior, purchase history, and other criteria. This enables you to deliver more targeted and relevant communications.

3. **Automated Workflows**: Leverage CoPilot's automation features to streamline CRM workflows. Automate tasks such as sending follow-up emails, scheduling appointments, and updating customer records.

4. **Multi-Channel Communication**: Manage customer interactions across multiple channels, including email, social media, live chat, and phone. CoPilot provides a unified platform to track and manage all communications.

5. **Customer Support Tools**: Use CoPilot's customer support tools to manage and resolve customer inquiries efficiently. Implement ticketing systems, live chat, and knowledge bases to provide comprehensive support.

6. **Analytics and Reporting**: CoPilot's analytics tools help you track key CRM metrics such as customer satisfaction, response times, and support ticket resolution rates. Use these insights to optimize your CRM strategies.

Enhancing Customer Data Management

Effective customer data management is the foundation of a successful CRM strategy. Here's how to manage customer data with CoPilot:

1. **Data Collection**: Collect customer data from various touchpoints, including website forms, social media interactions, and purchase history. Use CoPilot to integrate these data sources into a single platform.

2. **Data Organization**: Organize customer data into structured formats that are easy to analyze and use. Ensure that data is up-to-date and accurate.

3. **Data Analysis**: Use CoPilot's analytics tools to analyze customer data and identify patterns, trends, and insights. This information can help you understand customer behavior and preferences.

4. **Data Security**: Ensure that customer data is stored securely and complies with data protection regulations. CoPilot provides security features to protect sensitive information.

Customer Segmentation and Personalization

Customer segmentation allows you to tailor your marketing and communication efforts to specific groups within your customer base. Here's how to use CoPilot for segmentation and personalization:

1. **Identify Segments**: Use CoPilot to identify and create customer segments based on criteria such as demographics, purchase behavior, and engagement levels.

2. **Personalized Campaigns**: Develop personalized marketing campaigns for each segment. Use CoPilot's content generation tools to create targeted messages that resonate with each group.

3. **Tailored Offers**: Offer personalized promotions and discounts to different segments based on their purchase history and preferences.

4. **Behavioral Triggers**: Set up automated triggers to send personalized messages based

on customer actions, such as abandoned carts or recent purchases.

Improving Communication and Engagement

Maintaining regular and meaningful communication with your customers is key to building strong relationships. Here's how to enhance communication and engagement with CoPilot:

1. **Multi-Channel Communication**: Use CoPilot to manage customer interactions across various channels, ensuring a consistent and seamless experience.

2. **Personalized Emails**: Send personalized emails to different customer segments, addressing their specific needs and interests. Use CoPilot's email marketing tools to automate and optimize these communications.

3. **Social Media Engagement**: Engage with customers on social media platforms. Use CoPilot to monitor and respond to social media interactions, building stronger connections with your audience.

4. **Live Chat and Messaging**: Implement live chat and messaging features on your website to provide real-time support and engagement.

CoPilot's tools help you manage these interactions efficiently.

Providing Exceptional Customer Support

Exceptional customer support is essential for customer satisfaction and loyalty. Here's how to enhance your support efforts with CoPilot:

1. **Support Ticketing System**: Use CoPilot's ticketing system to manage and track customer support requests. Ensure that tickets are resolved promptly and effectively.

2. **Knowledge Base**: Create a comprehensive knowledge base with FAQs, tutorials, and troubleshooting guides. This self-service resource can help customers find answers to common issues.

3. **Live Chat Support**: Offer live chat support to provide immediate assistance to customers. CoPilot's live chat tools help you manage these interactions and resolve issues quickly.

4. **Customer Feedback**: Collect feedback from customers after support interactions to gauge satisfaction and identify areas for improvement.

Gathering and Analyzing Customer Feedback

Customer feedback provides valuable insights into how you can improve your products, services, and customer experience. Here's how to gather and analyze feedback with CoPilot:

1. **Surveys and Polls**: Use CoPilot to create and distribute surveys and polls to gather customer feedback. Ask specific questions to understand their needs and preferences.

2. **Feedback Forms**: Implement feedback forms on your website and in your emails to collect customer opinions and suggestions.

3. **Analyze Feedback**: Use CoPilot's analytics tools to analyze feedback and identify common themes and areas for improvement.

4. **Actionable Insights**: Translate feedback into actionable insights. Use this information to make data-driven decisions and enhance your products and services.

Practical Tips for CRM Success

To get the most out of your CRM efforts, consider the following practical tips:

1. **Consistent Follow-Up**: Follow up with customers regularly to maintain engagement and address any issues or concerns.

2. **Personal Touch**: Add a personal touch to your interactions. Address customers by their names and acknowledge their past interactions with your brand.

3. **Proactive Support**: Anticipate customer needs and offer proactive support. For example, provide guidance on using your products or offer assistance before customers ask for it.

4. **Continuous Improvement**: Regularly review and optimize your CRM strategies. Use data and feedback to continuously improve your customer interactions and experiences.

Conclusion

Enhancing your CRM efforts with CoPilot involves effective customer data management, segmentation and personalization, improved communication and engagement, exceptional customer support, and continuous feedback analysis. By leveraging CoPilot's powerful tools and features, you can build stronger relationships with your customers, increase loyalty, and drive business growth. In the next chapter, we will explore how to use CoPilot to create and manage effective content marketing strategies that engage your audience and drive traffic to your website.

Chapter 10: Creating and Managing Effective Content Marketing Strategies

Content marketing is a powerful way to engage your audience, build brand awareness, and drive traffic to your website. By providing valuable and relevant content, you can attract and retain customers, establish your brand as an authority, and support your overall marketing goals. In this chapter, we will explore how to use CoPilot to create and manage effective content marketing strategies that resonate with your audience and drive results.

The Importance of Content Marketing

Content marketing offers several benefits:

1. **Engagement**: High-quality content engages your audience and encourages them to interact with your brand.

2. **Brand Awareness**: Consistent content marketing helps increase your brand's visibility and recognition.

3. **SEO**: Optimized content improves your search engine rankings, driving organic traffic to your website.

4. **Authority and Trust**: Providing valuable content establishes your brand as an authority in your industry and builds trust with your audience.

5. **Lead Generation**: Content marketing can generate leads by attracting potential customers and guiding them through the sales funnel.

Key Elements of Content Marketing

To create effective content marketing strategies, focus on the following key elements:

1. **Content Strategy**: Develop a comprehensive content strategy that aligns with your business goals and audience needs.

2. **Content Creation**: Produce high-quality, valuable content that addresses your audience's pain points and interests.

3. **Content Distribution**: Distribute your content through various channels to reach a broader audience.

4. **SEO Optimization**: Optimize your content for search engines to improve visibility and drive organic traffic.

5. **Performance Measurement**: Track and analyze the performance of your content to continuously improve your strategies.

Developing Your Content Strategy

A well-defined content strategy is the foundation of successful content marketing. Here's how to develop your content strategy with CoPilot:

1. **Define Your Goals**: Start by defining the objectives of your content marketing efforts. Are you looking to increase brand awareness, generate leads, or drive sales? Clear goals will guide your strategy and help you measure success.

2. **Understand Your Audience**: Use CoPilot's audience insights to understand your target audience's needs, preferences, and pain points. This information will help you create content that resonates with them.

3. **Content Themes and Topics**: Identify key themes and topics that align with your audience's interests and your business goals.

Use CoPilot's keyword research tools to find relevant and high-performing topics.

4. **Content Calendar**: Create a content calendar to plan and schedule your content. This ensures a consistent and organized approach to content creation and distribution.

5. **Content Formats**: Determine the types of content that will best engage your audience, such as blog posts, articles, videos, infographics, and social media posts.

Creating High-Quality Content

Creating high-quality content is essential for engaging your audience and achieving your content marketing goals. Here's how to create valuable content with CoPilot:

1. **Research and Planning**: Conduct thorough research on your chosen topics to ensure accuracy and relevance. Use CoPilot's content planning tools to outline your content and organize your ideas.

2. **Content Creation**: Use CoPilot's content generation tools to create well-written, informative, and engaging content. Focus on

providing value to your audience by addressing their needs and interests.

3. **Visual Content**: Incorporate visuals such as images, infographics, and videos to enhance your content and make it more engaging. Use CoPilot's design tools to create high-quality visuals.

4. **SEO Optimization**: Optimize your content for search engines by incorporating relevant keywords, using proper headings, and creating meta descriptions. CoPilot's SEO tools can help you optimize your content for better visibility.

5. **Editing and Proofreading**: Ensure that your content is free of errors and flows smoothly. Use CoPilot's editing tools to review and refine your content before publishing.

Distributing Your Content

Effective content distribution is key to reaching a broader audience and maximizing the impact of your content. Here's how to distribute your content with CoPilot:

1. **Social Media**: Share your content on social media platforms to reach and engage with your audience. Use CoPilot's social media

management tools to schedule and track your posts.

2. **Email Marketing**: Distribute your content through email newsletters to keep your subscribers informed and engaged. Use CoPilot's email marketing tools to create and send targeted email campaigns.

3. **Content Syndication**: Syndicate your content on relevant platforms and websites to increase its reach and visibility. Use CoPilot to identify and connect with potential syndication partners.

4. **Guest Blogging**: Contribute guest posts to industry blogs and websites to expand your reach and build backlinks. Use CoPilot to identify guest blogging opportunities and manage your outreach efforts.

5. **Influencer Partnerships**: Collaborate with influencers to promote your content and reach a larger audience. Use CoPilot to identify and connect with relevant influencers in your industry.

Measuring Content Performance

Tracking and analyzing the performance of your content is essential for understanding its impact and optimizing your strategies. Here's how to measure content performance with CoPilot:

1. **Key Metrics**: Identify key metrics to track, such as page views, time on page, social shares, engagement rates, and conversion rates.

2. **Analytics Tools**: Use CoPilot's analytics tools to track and analyze the performance of your content. Monitor key metrics and identify trends and patterns.

3. **A/B Testing**: Conduct A/B tests to compare different versions of your content and determine which performs better. Use CoPilot's A/B testing tools to optimize your content based on the results.

4. **Feedback and Insights**: Gather feedback from your audience to understand their preferences and needs. Use CoPilot to collect and analyze feedback, and use these insights to improve your content.

5. **Continuous Improvement**: Regularly review and optimize your content marketing strategies based on performance data and feedback.

Continuously improve your content to ensure it remains relevant and valuable to your audience.

Practical Tips for Content Marketing Success

To get the most out of your content marketing efforts, consider the following practical tips:

1. **Consistency**: Consistently produce and publish high-quality content to keep your audience engaged and maintain your brand's visibility.

2. **Value-Driven Content**: Focus on providing value to your audience by addressing their needs, answering their questions, and solving their problems.

3. **Storytelling**: Use storytelling techniques to make your content more engaging and relatable. Share stories that resonate with your audience and highlight your brand's personality.

4. **Collaborate**: Collaborate with other brands, influencers, and industry experts to expand your reach and bring fresh perspectives to your content.

5. **Repurpose Content**: Repurpose existing content into different formats to reach a wider

audience. For example, turn a blog post into a video or an infographic.

Conclusion

Creating and managing effective content marketing strategies is essential for engaging your audience, building brand awareness, and driving traffic to your website. By leveraging CoPilot's powerful tools and features, you can develop a comprehensive content strategy, create high-quality content, distribute it effectively, and measure its performance to continuously improve your efforts. In the next chapter, we will explore how to use CoPilot to harness the power of social media marketing, connecting with your audience and driving engagement across various platforms.

Chapter 11: Harnessing the Power of Social Media Marketing

Social media marketing is a dynamic and powerful way to connect with your audience, build brand awareness, and drive engagement. By leveraging social media platforms, you can reach a broader audience, foster relationships, and create a vibrant online community. In this chapter, we will explore how to use CoPilot to harness the power of social media marketing, develop effective strategies, and achieve your marketing goals.

The Importance of Social Media Marketing

Social media marketing offers several benefits:

1. **Audience Reach**: Social media platforms have vast user bases, allowing you to reach a large and diverse audience.

2. **Engagement**: Social media facilitates direct interaction with your audience, fostering engagement and building relationships.

3. **Brand Awareness**: Regular social media activity increases your brand's visibility and recognition.

4. **Traffic Generation**: Social media can drive significant traffic to your website and other online assets.

5. **Customer Insights**: Social media provides valuable insights into your audience's preferences, behaviors, and feedback.

Key Elements of Social Media Marketing

To harness the power of social media marketing, focus on the following key elements:

1. **Strategy Development**: Create a comprehensive social media strategy that aligns with your business goals and audience preferences.

2. **Content Creation**: Produce engaging and shareable content that resonates with your audience.

3. **Platform Selection**: Choose the social media platforms that best suit your brand and audience.

4. **Community Management**: Foster a vibrant online community by engaging with your audience and responding to their interactions.

5. **Performance Measurement**: Track and analyze the performance of your social media activities to optimize your strategies.

Developing Your Social Media Strategy

A well-defined social media strategy is essential for effective social media marketing. Here's how to develop your strategy with CoPilot:

1. **Define Your Goals**: Start by defining the objectives of your social media marketing efforts. Are you looking to increase brand

awareness, drive traffic, generate leads, or boost sales? Clear goals will guide your strategy and help you measure success.

2. **Understand Your Audience**: Use CoPilot's audience insights to understand your target audience's demographics, interests, and behaviors. This information will help you create content that resonates with them.

3. **Platform Selection**: Choose the social media platforms that best align with your audience and goals. Popular platforms include Facebook, Instagram, Twitter, LinkedIn, and Pinterest.

4. **Content Plan**: Develop a content plan that outlines the types of content you will create, the themes you will focus on, and the frequency of your posts. Use CoPilot's content planning tools to organize and schedule your content.

5. **Engagement Tactics**: Plan how you will engage with your audience, including responding to comments, participating in discussions, and running social media campaigns and contests.

Creating Engaging Social Media Content

Creating engaging content is key to successful social media marketing. Here's how to create compelling social media content with CoPilot:

1. **Visual Content**: Use images, videos, infographics, and other visual elements to capture attention and make your content more engaging. CoPilot's design tools can help you create high-quality visuals.

2. **Storytelling**: Share stories that resonate with your audience and highlight your brand's personality. Use CoPilot's content generation tools to craft compelling stories.

3. **User-Generated Content**: Encourage your audience to create and share content related to your brand. User-generated content can increase engagement and build community.

4. **Interactive Content**: Create interactive content such as polls, quizzes, and live videos to engage your audience and encourage participation.

5. **Value-Driven Content**: Provide value to your audience by sharing informative, educational, and entertaining content. Address their needs, answer their questions, and solve their problems.

Managing Your Social Media Presence

Effective management of your social media presence is crucial for building a strong online community. Here's how to manage your social media presence with CoPilot:

1. **Content Scheduling**: Use CoPilot's social media management tools to schedule your posts in advance. This ensures a consistent posting schedule and saves time.

2. **Engagement Monitoring**: Monitor your social media channels for comments, mentions, and messages. Use CoPilot to track and respond to interactions in a timely manner.

3. **Community Building**: Foster a sense of community by engaging with your audience, responding to their comments, and participating in discussions. Encourage user-generated content and recognize your most active followers.

4. **Social Listening**: Use CoPilot's social listening tools to monitor conversations about your brand, industry, and competitors. Social listening helps you stay informed about trends,

gather feedback, and identify opportunities for engagement.

Running Social Media Campaigns

Social media campaigns are targeted efforts to achieve specific marketing goals, such as promoting a product launch, increasing brand awareness, or driving sales. Here's how to run effective social media campaigns with CoPilot:

1. **Campaign Goals**: Define clear goals for your campaign. What do you want to achieve? Set specific, measurable, achievable, relevant, and time-bound (SMART) objectives.

2. **Target Audience**: Identify the target audience for your campaign. Use CoPilot's audience segmentation tools to create detailed audience profiles and tailor your messages to their preferences.

3. **Creative Content**: Develop creative content that aligns with your campaign goals and resonates with your target audience. Use CoPilot's content creation tools to produce engaging visuals, videos, and copy.

4. **Promotion Plan**: Plan how you will promote your campaign across different social media

platforms. Consider using paid ads to reach a wider audience and boost your campaign's visibility.

5. **Engagement Strategy**: Engage with your audience throughout the campaign. Respond to comments, encourage participation, and use interactive elements such as polls and contests to drive engagement.

6. **Performance Tracking**: Monitor the performance of your campaign using CoPilot's analytics tools. Track key metrics such as reach, engagement, click-through rates, and conversions. Adjust your strategy based on the insights gained.

Leveraging Influencer Partnerships

Influencer partnerships can amplify your social media reach and enhance your brand's credibility. Here's how to leverage influencer partnerships with CoPilot:

1. **Identify Influencers**: Use CoPilot to identify influencers who align with your brand and have a strong following within your target audience. Consider factors such as engagement rates, authenticity, and relevance.

2. **Outreach and Collaboration**: Reach out to influencers with a personalized pitch that highlights the benefits of collaborating with your brand. Use CoPilot to manage outreach and communication with influencers.

3. **Co-Create Content**: Collaborate with influencers to create authentic and engaging content that resonates with their audience. Ensure that the content aligns with your brand's messaging and goals.

4. **Campaign Integration**: Integrate influencer content into your broader social media strategy. Promote the content across your own channels and encourage your audience to engage with it.

5. **Track Performance**: Use CoPilot's analytics tools to track the performance of influencer partnerships. Measure the impact on reach, engagement, and conversions. Use these insights to optimize future collaborations.

Measuring and Analyzing Social Media Performance

Measuring and analyzing the performance of your social media efforts is essential for continuous improvement. Here's how to measure and analyze social media performance with CoPilot:

1. **Define Key Metrics**: Identify the key metrics that align with your social media goals. Common metrics include reach, engagement, follower growth, click-through rates, and conversions.

2. **Use Analytics Tools**: Use CoPilot's analytics tools to track and analyze these metrics across different social media platforms. Gain insights into what's working and what needs improvement.

3. **A/B Testing**: Conduct A/B tests to compare different versions of your social media content, ads, and campaigns. Use the results to optimize your strategies and improve performance.

4. **Benchmarking**: Compare your social media performance against industry benchmarks and competitors. Use CoPilot to identify areas where you excel and opportunities for growth.

5. **Continuous Improvement**: Regularly review your social media performance and make data-driven adjustments to your strategies. Use the

insights gained to continuously improve your social media marketing efforts.

Practical Tips for Social Media Marketing Success

To get the most out of your social media marketing efforts, consider the following practical tips:

1. **Consistency**: Maintain a consistent posting schedule to keep your audience engaged and maintain your brand's visibility.

2. **Authenticity**: Be authentic in your interactions and content. Authenticity builds trust and fosters stronger connections with your audience.

3. **Engagement**: Actively engage with your audience by responding to comments, participating in discussions, and encouraging user-generated content.

4. **Trends**: Stay updated on social media trends and best practices. Use CoPilot's resources to keep informed and implement the latest strategies.

5. **Flexibility**: Be flexible and adaptable in your social media strategies. Monitor performance

and make adjustments based on what's working and what's not.

Conclusion

Harnessing the power of social media marketing involves developing a comprehensive strategy, creating engaging content, effectively managing your presence, running targeted campaigns, leveraging influencer partnerships, and continuously measuring and optimizing performance. By leveraging CoPilot's powerful tools and features, you can streamline your social media efforts, connect with your audience, and achieve your marketing goals. In the next chapter, we will explore how to leverage CoPilot's advanced features to gain deeper insights and optimize your overall marketing strategy.

Chapter 12: Leveraging Advanced Features of CoPilot

CoPilot offers a range of advanced features designed to provide deeper insights, optimize marketing strategies, and drive better results. In this chapter, we will explore how to leverage these advanced features to enhance your marketing efforts and achieve your business goals.

The Importance of Advanced Marketing Tools

Advanced marketing tools are essential for:

1. **Deeper Insights**: Gaining a more comprehensive understanding of your audience, performance metrics, and market trends.

2. **Strategic Optimization**: Making data-driven decisions to optimize your marketing strategies and improve ROI.

3. **Competitive Advantage**: Staying ahead of competitors by leveraging the latest tools and technologies.

4. **Efficiency**: Streamlining marketing processes and saving time with automation and advanced analytics.

Key Advanced Features of CoPilot

CoPilot offers several advanced features that can enhance your marketing efforts:

1. **Predictive Analytics**: Using AI to predict future trends, customer behavior, and campaign outcomes.

2. **Advanced Segmentation**: Creating highly detailed audience segments based on multiple criteria for more targeted marketing.

3. **Marketing Automation**: Automating complex marketing workflows to increase efficiency and effectiveness.

4. **Custom Reporting**: Creating customized reports to track specific metrics and gain actionable insights.

5. **Integration Capabilities**: Integrating CoPilot with other marketing tools and platforms for a seamless marketing ecosystem.

Using Predictive Analytics

Predictive analytics leverages AI to forecast future trends and behaviors based on historical data. Here's how to use predictive analytics with CoPilot:

1. **Data Collection**: Ensure you have comprehensive data from various sources, including customer interactions, sales, and market trends.

2. **Predictive Models**: Use CoPilot's predictive models to analyze this data and identify patterns. The models can predict future

customer behavior, campaign performance, and market trends.

3. **Strategic Planning**: Use the insights gained from predictive analytics to inform your strategic planning. For example, anticipate customer needs, optimize inventory levels, and plan marketing campaigns.

4. **Risk Management**: Identify potential risks and opportunities based on predictive insights. Use this information to make proactive decisions and mitigate risks.

Advanced Audience Segmentation

Advanced audience segmentation allows you to create highly targeted marketing campaigns. Here's how to leverage advanced segmentation with CoPilot:

1. **Multi-Criteria Segmentation**: Segment your audience based on multiple criteria, such as demographics, behavior, purchase history, and engagement levels.

2. **Lookalike Audiences**: Create lookalike audiences based on your best-performing segments. Use CoPilot to identify and target new potential customers who share similar characteristics.

3. **Dynamic Segmentation**: Use CoPilot to create dynamic segments that automatically update based on real-time data. This ensures your segments are always current and relevant.

4. **Personalized Campaigns**: Develop personalized marketing campaigns for each segment. Use CoPilot's content generation tools to create tailored messages that resonate with each group.

Marketing Automation

Marketing automation streamlines your marketing processes and increases efficiency. Here's how to use marketing automation with CoPilot:

1. **Automated Workflows**: Set up automated workflows for tasks such as email marketing, social media posting, lead nurturing, and customer follow-up. CoPilot's automation tools help you create and manage these workflows.

2. **Trigger-Based Automation**: Use triggers to automate actions based on specific customer behaviors, such as website visits, form submissions, and purchase history.

3. **Drip Campaigns**: Create automated drip campaigns to nurture leads over time. Use

CoPilot to design and schedule a series of emails that guide prospects through the sales funnel.

4. **Performance Monitoring**: Monitor the performance of your automated workflows using CoPilot's analytics tools. Make adjustments as needed to optimize results.

Custom Reporting

Custom reporting allows you to track specific metrics and gain actionable insights. Here's how to create custom reports with CoPilot:

1. **Identify Key Metrics**: Determine the key metrics you need to track based on your business goals and marketing strategies.

2. **Custom Dashboards**: Use CoPilot to create custom dashboards that display your key metrics in a clear and actionable format. Customize your dashboards to suit your specific needs.

3. **Regular Reporting**: Schedule regular reports to be generated and delivered to your team. Use these reports to track progress, identify trends, and make data-driven decisions.

4. **Data Visualization**: Use CoPilot's data visualization tools to create charts, graphs, and other visual representations of your data. This makes it easier to interpret and communicate insights.

Integration Capabilities

Integrating CoPilot with other marketing tools and platforms creates a seamless marketing ecosystem. Here's how to leverage integration capabilities with CoPilot:

1. **API Integration**: Use CoPilot's API to integrate with other marketing tools, such as CRM systems, email marketing platforms, and analytics tools.

2. **Data Syncing**: Ensure that data is synced across all integrated platforms. This provides a unified view of your marketing activities and performance.

3. **Workflow Integration**: Integrate CoPilot into your existing workflows to streamline processes and increase efficiency. Use CoPilot to automate tasks and manage campaigns across multiple platforms.

4. **Third-Party Tools**: Explore CoPilot's marketplace for third-party tools and integrations that can enhance your marketing efforts. Use these tools to extend CoPilot's capabilities and tailor it to your specific needs.

Practical Tips for Leveraging Advanced Features

To get the most out of CoPilot's advanced features, consider the following practical tips:

1. **Continuous Learning**: Stay updated on the latest features and best practices for using CoPilot. Regularly explore CoPilot's resources and training materials.

2. **Experimentation**: Experiment with different features and strategies to see what works best for your business. Use A/B testing and data analysis to refine your approach.

3. **Collaboration**: Involve your team in leveraging CoPilot's advanced features. Collaborate on strategy development, campaign management, and performance analysis.

4. **Feedback Loop**: Establish a feedback loop to continuously gather input from your team and customers. Use this feedback to improve your marketing efforts and CoPilot usage.

Conclusion

Leveraging CoPilot's advanced features can provide deeper insights, optimize your marketing strategies, and drive better results. By using predictive analytics, advanced audience segmentation, marketing automation, custom reporting, and integration capabilities, you can enhance your marketing efforts and achieve your business goals. In the next chapter, we will explore how to use CoPilot to develop effective influencer marketing strategies and partnerships, expanding your reach and building brand credibility.

Chapter 13: Developing Effective Influencer Marketing Strategies

Influencer marketing has become a powerful way to reach new audiences, build brand credibility, and drive engagement. By partnering with influencers, you can leverage their reach and influence to promote your brand and connect with their followers. In this chapter, we will explore how to use CoPilot to develop effective influencer marketing strategies, identify the right influencers, and measure the impact of your partnerships.

The Importance of Influencer Marketing

Influencer marketing offers several benefits:

1. **Increased Reach**: Influencers have established audiences that can significantly extend your brand's reach.

2. **Credibility and Trust**: Influencers are trusted by their followers, lending credibility to your brand when they endorse your products or services.

3. **Engagement**: Influencer content tends to generate high levels of engagement, driving more interactions with your brand.

4. **Targeted Marketing**: Influencers often have niche audiences, allowing you to target specific demographics and interests.

5. **Content Creation**: Influencers can create high-quality content that resonates with their audience and aligns with your brand's messaging.

Identifying the Right Influencers

Finding the right influencers is crucial for the success of your influencer marketing strategy. Here's how to identify the right influencers with CoPilot:

1. **Define Your Goals**: Start by defining the goals of your influencer marketing campaign. Are you

looking to increase brand awareness, drive traffic, generate leads, or boost sales? Clear goals will guide your influencer selection process.

2. **Audience Alignment**: Ensure that the influencer's audience aligns with your target audience. Use CoPilot's audience insights to identify influencers who have followers that match your customer demographics and interests.

3. **Engagement Metrics**: Look beyond follower count and consider engagement metrics such as likes, comments, and shares. Influencers with high engagement rates tend to have more active and involved audiences.

4. **Content Relevance**: Review the influencer's content to ensure it aligns with your brand's values and messaging. The content should be relevant to your industry and resonate with your target audience.

5. **Authenticity**: Choose influencers who are authentic and have a genuine connection with their audience. Authentic influencers are more likely to drive meaningful engagement and conversions.

Developing Influencer Partnerships

Building strong partnerships with influencers involves clear communication, collaboration, and mutual benefit. Here's how to develop effective influencer partnerships with CoPilot:

1. **Outreach**: Use CoPilot to manage influencer outreach. Craft personalized messages that highlight the benefits of collaborating with your brand. Be clear about your campaign goals and expectations.

2. **Collaboration**: Collaborate with influencers to co-create content that aligns with your brand's messaging and resonates with their audience. Provide creative freedom while ensuring the content meets your guidelines.

3. **Compensation**: Determine a fair compensation structure for your influencers. This could include monetary payment, free products, affiliate commissions, or a combination of these.

4. **Contracts and Agreements**: Formalize your partnerships with contracts that outline the terms of the collaboration, including deliverables, timelines, compensation, and disclosure requirements.

5. **Ongoing Communication**: Maintain regular communication with your influencers throughout the campaign. Provide feedback, address any concerns, and support their efforts to promote your brand.

Measuring the Impact of Influencer Campaigns

Tracking and analyzing the performance of your influencer campaigns is essential for understanding their impact and optimizing future efforts. Here's how to measure the impact of influencer campaigns with CoPilot:

1. **Key Metrics**: Identify key metrics to track, such as reach, engagement, website traffic, conversions, and return on investment (ROI).

2. **Custom Tracking Links**: Use custom tracking links to monitor the traffic and conversions generated by each influencer. This helps you attribute results accurately.

3. **Performance Reports**: Use CoPilot to create detailed performance reports that track the progress of your influencer campaigns. Analyze the data to identify trends, successes, and areas for improvement.

4. **ROI Calculation**: Calculate the ROI of your influencer campaigns by comparing the revenue generated to the total cost of the campaigns. Use this information to assess the effectiveness of your influencer partnerships.

5. **Feedback and Improvement**: Gather feedback from your influencers and analyze the performance data to identify areas for improvement. Use these insights to refine your influencer marketing strategies and optimize future campaigns.

Practical Tips for Influencer Marketing Success

To get the most out of your influencer marketing efforts, consider the following practical tips:

1. **Long-Term Relationships**: Focus on building long-term relationships with influencers rather than one-off collaborations. Long-term partnerships tend to be more authentic and effective.

2. **Transparency**: Be transparent with your influencers about your expectations, goals, and compensation. Clear communication builds trust and ensures a smooth collaboration.

3. **Diverse Influencers**: Collaborate with a diverse range of influencers to reach different segments of your target audience. Consider working with macro, micro, and nano influencers.

4. **Content Guidelines**: Provide clear content guidelines to ensure that the influencer's content aligns with your brand's messaging and values. However, allow creative freedom to maintain authenticity.

5. **Engage with Influencer Content**: Actively engage with the content created by your influencers. Share, like, and comment on their posts to show appreciation and amplify their reach.

Conclusion

Developing effective influencer marketing strategies involves identifying the right influencers, building strong partnerships, creating compelling content, and measuring the impact of your campaigns. By leveraging CoPilot's powerful tools and features, you can streamline your influencer marketing efforts, connect with the right influencers, and achieve your marketing goals. In the next chapter, we will explore how to use CoPilot to analyze market trends and competitor strategies, helping you stay ahead of the competition and make informed business decisions.

Chapter 14: Analyzing Market Trends and Competitor Strategies

Understanding market trends and competitor strategies is crucial for staying ahead in a competitive business landscape. By analyzing these factors, you can make informed decisions, identify opportunities, and develop strategies that give you a competitive edge. In this chapter, we will explore how to use CoPilot to analyze market trends and competitor strategies, helping you navigate the market effectively and achieve your business goals.

The Importance of Market Analysis

Market analysis offers several benefits:

1. **Informed Decisions**: Gain insights into market trends, customer preferences, and competitive dynamics to make data-driven decisions.

2. **Opportunity Identification**: Identify emerging opportunities, such as new market segments, product trends, and untapped customer needs.

3. **Risk Mitigation**: Anticipate market changes and potential risks, allowing you to adapt your strategies proactively.

4. **Competitive Advantage**: Understand your competitors' strengths and weaknesses to develop strategies that differentiate your brand and capitalize on their gaps.

5. **Strategic Planning**: Use market insights to inform your long-term strategic planning and ensure your business remains relevant and competitive.

Using CoPilot to Analyze Market Trends

CoPilot provides tools and features to help you analyze market trends effectively. Here's how to use CoPilot for market analysis:

1. **Data Collection**: Collect data from various sources, including industry reports, market research, customer feedback, and social media. CoPilot's data integration capabilities allow you to gather and centralize this information.

2. **Trend Analysis**: Use CoPilot's analytics tools to identify and analyze market trends. Look for patterns in customer behavior, product demand, and industry developments.

3. **Customer Insights**: Analyze customer feedback and reviews to understand their preferences, pain points, and emerging needs. Use CoPilot to gather and analyze this data.

4. **Competitor Monitoring**: Monitor your competitors' activities, product launches, and marketing campaigns. Use CoPilot to track their social media presence, website updates, and industry news.

5. **Predictive Analytics**: Leverage CoPilot's predictive analytics to forecast future market trends and customer behavior. Use these insights to inform your strategic planning and decision-making.

Understanding Competitor Strategies

Analyzing your competitors' strategies provides valuable insights into their strengths, weaknesses, and market positioning. Here's how to understand competitor strategies with CoPilot:

1. **Competitor Identification**: Identify your key competitors within your industry. Use CoPilot to gather information on their products, services, pricing, and market positioning.

2. **SWOT Analysis**: Conduct a SWOT analysis (Strengths, Weaknesses, Opportunities, Threats) of your competitors. Use CoPilot to gather data and insights to support your analysis.

3. **Marketing Strategies**: Analyze your competitors' marketing strategies, including their advertising campaigns, content marketing, social media presence, and customer engagement tactics.

4. **Product Analysis**: Evaluate your competitors' product offerings, including features, pricing, and customer reviews. Use CoPilot to track product updates and new launches.

5. **Customer Feedback**: Monitor customer feedback and reviews of your competitors. Identify common complaints, preferences, and areas where your competitors excel or fall short.

Leveraging Market and Competitor Insights

Use the insights gained from market and competitor analysis to develop and refine your business strategies. Here's how to leverage these insights with CoPilot:

1. **Strategic Planning**: Incorporate market and competitor insights into your strategic

planning. Use the data to identify growth opportunities, mitigate risks, and differentiate your brand.

2. **Product Development**: Use customer feedback and market trends to inform your product development efforts. Focus on addressing unmet needs and enhancing your product offerings.

3. **Marketing Campaigns**: Develop marketing campaigns that capitalize on market opportunities and address competitive gaps. Use CoPilot to create targeted and impactful campaigns.

4. **Pricing Strategies**: Adjust your pricing strategies based on competitor analysis and market demand. Ensure your pricing is competitive while maintaining profitability.

5. **Customer Experience**: Enhance your customer experience by addressing common pain points and incorporating best practices from competitors. Use CoPilot to gather feedback and measure satisfaction.

Practical Tips for Market and Competitor Analysis

To get the most out of your market and competitor analysis efforts, consider the following practical tips:

1. **Regular Monitoring**: Continuously monitor market trends and competitor activities. Regular analysis ensures you stay informed and can adapt quickly to changes.

2. **Comprehensive Data**: Use a variety of data sources to gain a holistic view of the market. Combine quantitative data with qualitative insights for a comprehensive analysis.

3. **Actionable Insights**: Focus on identifying actionable insights that can inform your strategies and decision-making. Prioritize insights that align with your business goals.

4. **Collaboration**: Involve your team in the analysis process. Collaborate to gather diverse perspectives and ensure a thorough understanding of the market landscape.

5. **Continuous Improvement**: Use the insights gained from market and competitor analysis to continuously improve your products, services, and marketing strategies. Stay agile and responsive to market changes.

Conclusion

Analyzing market trends and competitor strategies is essential for making informed decisions, identifying opportunities, and staying ahead of the competition. By leveraging CoPilot's powerful tools and features, you can gather valuable insights, develop data-driven strategies, and achieve your business goals. In the next chapter, we will explore ethical considerations in AI marketing, ensuring that your use of AI aligns with ethical standards and best practices.

Chapter 15: Ethical Considerations in AI Marketing

As AI continues to play a significant role in marketing, it's essential to consider the ethical implications of using AI-driven tools and strategies. Ethical AI marketing involves ensuring transparency, fairness, and accountability in your marketing practices. In this chapter, we will explore the key ethical considerations in AI marketing and how to use CoPilot responsibly and ethically.

The Importance of Ethical AI Marketing

Ethical AI marketing is crucial for several reasons:

1. **Trust and Credibility**: Ethical marketing practices build trust and credibility with your audience, fostering long-term relationships.

2. **Legal Compliance**: Adhering to ethical standards helps ensure compliance with data protection and privacy regulations.

3. **Fairness and Inclusivity**: Ethical AI marketing promotes fairness and inclusivity, avoiding biases and discrimination.

4. **Reputation Management**: Responsible use of AI protects your brand's reputation and prevents potential backlash from unethical practices.

5. **Sustainable Practices**: Ethical AI marketing supports sustainable business practices that benefit both your organization and society.

Key Ethical Considerations in AI Marketing

To ensure ethical AI marketing, consider the following key considerations:

1. **Transparency**: Be transparent about the use of AI in your marketing practices. Clearly communicate how AI is used to collect, analyze, and use customer data.

2. **Data Privacy**: Respect customer privacy by collecting and using data responsibly. Obtain

explicit consent for data collection and provide clear opt-out options.

3. **Bias and Fairness**: Address and mitigate biases in AI algorithms to ensure fair and unbiased marketing practices. Regularly audit AI models for potential biases and take corrective actions.

4. **Accountability**: Establish clear accountability for AI-driven marketing decisions. Ensure that there is human oversight and responsibility for AI actions.

5. **Ethical Data Use**: Use customer data ethically and responsibly. Avoid using data for purposes that customers have not explicitly agreed to or that could harm them.

Implementing Ethical AI Marketing with CoPilot

CoPilot provides tools and features that can help you implement ethical AI marketing practices. Here's how to use CoPilot responsibly and ethically:

1. **Data Transparency**: Use CoPilot to create transparent data collection and usage policies. Clearly communicate these policies to your customers and obtain their consent.

2. **Privacy Controls**: Implement strong privacy controls using CoPilot's data management tools. Ensure that customer data is stored securely and used only for its intended purposes.

3. **Bias Mitigation**: Use CoPilot's analytics tools to regularly audit AI models for biases. Implement strategies to mitigate biases and ensure fair treatment of all customer segments.

4. **Human Oversight**: Maintain human oversight of AI-driven marketing decisions. Use CoPilot's reporting and analytics tools to review and approve AI-generated content and strategies.

5. **Ethical Guidelines**: Develop and adhere to ethical guidelines for AI marketing. Use CoPilot to ensure that all marketing practices align with these guidelines and ethical standards.

Addressing Common Ethical Challenges

Addressing common ethical challenges in AI marketing is essential for maintaining trust and credibility. Here are some common challenges and how to address them with CoPilot:

1. **Data Privacy Concerns**: Address data privacy concerns by being transparent about data

collection and usage. Use CoPilot's privacy controls to protect customer data and ensure compliance with regulations.

2. **Algorithmic Bias**: Mitigate algorithmic bias by regularly auditing AI models and implementing corrective measures. Use CoPilot to monitor and address biases in your marketing strategies.

3. **Lack of Transparency**: Ensure transparency by clearly communicating how AI is used in your marketing practices. Use CoPilot to provide detailed explanations and obtain customer consent.

4. **Unintended Consequences**: Anticipate and address unintended consequences of AI marketing. Use CoPilot's analytics tools to monitor the impact of AI-driven decisions and make necessary adjustments.

5. **Ethical Dilemmas**: Navigate ethical dilemmas by adhering to your ethical guidelines and seeking input from diverse perspectives. Use CoPilot to ensure that all marketing practices align with ethical standards.

Practical Tips for Ethical AI Marketing

To implement ethical AI marketing effectively, consider the following practical tips:

1. **Educate Your Team**: Educate your team on the ethical implications of AI marketing. Provide training on ethical standards, data privacy, and bias mitigation.

2. **Engage with Customers**: Engage with your customers to understand their concerns and preferences regarding AI marketing. Use CoPilot to gather feedback and address customer concerns.

3. **Regular Audits**: Conduct regular audits of your AI-driven marketing practices to ensure compliance with ethical standards. Use CoPilot to monitor and report on ethical practices.

4. **Continuous Improvement**: Continuously improve your ethical AI marketing practices based on feedback and insights. Use CoPilot to implement best practices and stay updated on ethical standards.

5. **Collaboration**: Collaborate with industry experts, regulators, and stakeholders to stay informed about ethical standards and best

practices. Use CoPilot to ensure your marketing practices align with industry guidelines.

Conclusion

Ethical considerations in AI marketing are essential for building trust, ensuring compliance, and promoting fairness and inclusivity. By leveraging CoPilot's powerful tools and features responsibly and ethically, you can implement transparent, fair, and accountable marketing practices. This commitment to ethical AI marketing will enhance your brand's credibility, protect customer trust, and support sustainable business practices. In the final chapter, we will conclude our journey with CoPilot and outline the next steps for continuing to enhance your marketing strategies and achieve business growth.

Conclusion and Next Steps

Marketing your business with CoPilot has the potential to transform your marketing strategies, streamline processes, and drive significant growth. Throughout this book, we have explored various aspects of leveraging CoPilot's powerful tools and features to enhance your marketing efforts. As we conclude this journey, let's summarize the key takeaways and outline the next steps for continuing to enhance your marketing strategies and achieve business growth.

Key Takeaways

1. **Comprehensive Marketing**: CoPilot offers a comprehensive suite of tools to manage and optimize various aspects of your marketing efforts, from content creation and social media management to email marketing and CRM.

2. **Data-Driven Decisions**: Leveraging CoPilot's analytics and reporting tools allows you to make data-driven decisions, optimizing your strategies and improving your ROI.

3. **Automation and Efficiency**: CoPilot's automation features streamline marketing processes, saving time and resources while increasing efficiency and effectiveness.

4. **Personalization and Engagement**: CoPilot's audience insights and segmentation tools enable you to deliver personalized and engaging marketing campaigns that resonate with your target audience.

5. **Ethical Marketing**: Implementing ethical AI marketing practices with CoPilot ensures

transparency, fairness, and accountability, building trust and credibility with your audience.

Next Steps

To continue enhancing your marketing strategies with CoPilot, follow these next steps:

1. **Ongoing Learning and Improvement**: Stay updated on the latest features and best practices for using CoPilot. Regularly explore CoPilot's resources, training materials, and industry updates

Please continue writing.

1/2

ChatGPT

to ensure you're leveraging the tool to its fullest potential.

2. **Regular Performance Reviews**: Conduct regular reviews of your marketing performance using CoPilot's analytics and reporting tools. Identify areas for improvement and adjust your strategies based on data-driven insights.

3. **Experimentation and Innovation**: Continuously experiment with new strategies, content types, and marketing channels. Use

CoPilot's A/B testing and predictive analytics to refine your approaches and stay ahead of market trends.

4. **Customer Feedback**: Actively seek and incorporate customer feedback into your marketing efforts

4. **Customer Feedback**: Actively seek and incorporate customer feedback into your marketing efforts. Use CoPilot's feedback and survey tools to gather insights and make informed decisions that enhance the customer experience.

5. **Collaboration and Team Engagement**: Involve your marketing team in using CoPilot's tools and features. Encourage collaboration and share insights across your team to ensure everyone is aligned with your marketing goals and strategies.

6. **Integration with Other Tools**: Integrate CoPilot with other marketing tools and platforms you use. This seamless integration will help you create a unified marketing ecosystem, improving efficiency and effectiveness.

7. **Focus on Ethics and Compliance**: Maintain a strong focus on ethical AI marketing practices. Regularly review your strategies to ensure they are transparent, fair, and comply with data protection and privacy regulations.

8. **Continuous Content Creation**: Keep your content fresh and relevant by regularly producing new and engaging material. Use CoPilot's content generation tools to create a steady stream of high-quality content that resonates with your audience.

9. **Advanced Segmentation and Personalization**: Leverage CoPilot's advanced segmentation and personalization features to create highly targeted marketing campaigns. Tailor your messages to specific audience segments to increase engagement and conversions.

10. **Future-Proof Your Strategies**: Stay ahead of industry trends and technological advancements. Use CoPilot's predictive analytics and market insights to anticipate changes and adapt your strategies accordingly.

Final Thoughts

Marketing your business with CoPilot offers a powerful way to streamline your efforts, make data-driven decisions, and achieve significant growth. By utilizing CoPilot's comprehensive suite of tools, you can enhance every aspect of your marketing strategy, from content creation and social media management to CRM and advanced analytics.

Remember, the key to successful marketing lies in continuous learning, experimentation, and adaptation. Keep exploring new possibilities, leveraging data insights, and refining your strategies to stay ahead of the competition and meet your business goals.

Thank you for embarking on this journey with CoPilot. We hope this guide has provided valuable insights and practical steps to help you maximize your marketing efforts. As you continue to evolve and grow your business, CoPilot will be there to support you every step of the way, empowering you to achieve your marketing objectives and drive lasting success.

Resources for Continued Learning

To further enhance your knowledge and skills, consider exploring the following resources:

1. **CoPilot's Help Center**: Access detailed guides, tutorials, and FAQs to help you navigate and make the most of CoPilot's features.

2. **Online Courses**: Enroll in online courses and webinars focused on digital marketing, AI in marketing, and advanced analytics to stay updated with the latest trends and best practices.

3. **Industry Blogs and Publications**: Follow leading marketing blogs and publications to gain insights from industry experts and stay informed about new developments and strategies.

4. **Networking and Community Engagement**: Join marketing communities and forums to connect with other professionals, share experiences, and learn from each other's successes and challenges.

By leveraging these resources and continuously refining your marketing strategies, you'll be well-equipped to navigate the dynamic landscape of digital marketing and drive your business toward greater success with CoPilot.

Terry Power

www.ingramcontent.com/pod-product-compliance
Lightning Source LLC
LaVergne TN
LVHW022351060326
832902LV00022B/4380